Boudica:

Queen of the Iceni

Women of War - Book 1

History Nerds

Boudica: Queen of the Iceni

Women of War - Book 1

Table of Contents

Introduction

All throughout history we read of so many people that turned the tide of battle. Men and women that changed history for the better, that stamped their names on the history books and left the world in no doubt who they were.

In this series we want to focus on the mighty women of war. What made them stand out above the rest? How did they change the face of battle?

As we delve into this series we want to draw our eyes to women that when faced with horrific circumstances, refused to go silently into the night. The women we will look at were ordinary women that found a deep strength hidden in themselves. They were women that rose to the challenge of defending their people, of making a difference, of showing that being feminine is a blessing.

We intend to draw your attention to queens, to spies, to leaders of armies and much more.

Most importantly we want to show you that the very fabric that made these women change history, is knitted into each and every woman. Every leader, every teacher, every adventurer, every housewife, mother and child.

Rightly it is said that "hell hath no fury like a woman scorned" for when the Romans came to England they met Boudica, when the French needed hope they had Joan of Arc, when Jewish children needed rescue they had Irena Sendler. But for this book we want to focus on Boudica, Queen of the Iceni.

Nothing is as strong as the desire for *freedom*. The peoples who were oppressed by the ever-expanding Roman Empire were sure to know this, seeing their heritage, their lands and families, destroyed in the wake of this powerful conquering torrent. Amongst these were the Ancient Britons, peoples with Celtic origins that dwelt in what are today England, Scotland, Wales, and Cornwall. Unable to hold their ground before such a powerful force, they suffered a tragic fate. Falling under the shadow of the Roman Empire, they were quickly subdued and subjected to a hard and humiliating occupation. For many years they saw their lives and cultures dissipating under the oppressive heel of the conquerors, and prayed in secret for a brave and powerful leader that would bring back their lost glory. In time, such a leader did appear: *Queen Boudica of the Iceni.*

Rising from oppression and defeat, this brave woman of war stood in front of her people, her courage unshaken, raising high up the banner of the conquered Britons. Driven by her unfailing will, by the suffering of her people, and the desire to cast away the shackles of the Roman Empire, this she-warrior stood boldly in front of the Briton tribes and led them in revolt. Ultimately, she paid the highest price, laying down her life at the altar of freedom. But her struggle gained her a place amongst the greatest of Britain's heroes and heroines, etching her name into the foundations of this nation's glorious history. Boudica's revolt began a long struggle towards independence, and ensured that she and all those who laid their lives besides her, live forever in our memories. This is the story of a noble woman of war - the story of Boudica.

Chapter I:
The Roman Conquest of Britain

From meager origins as a dominant Iron Age city-state from Latium in Italy, Rome rose to the greatest heights of power. Home of the Latins, this city ascended upon an eternal path of war - a path that it never truly left. At first conquering the neighboring Italic tribes, Rome became an influential Kingdom, then a Republic, and finally an Empire. Over the centuries, its borders continually expanded: first across the Italian Peninsula, the Mediterranean, Spain and North Africa, to Asia Minor, Central Europe, and finally to the British Isles. The Roman Empire was amongst the largest powers on Earth, and it always wanted *more*.

In time, the leaders of Rome cast their glance upon the Isles of the Britons, an area that was seen at the time as a remote place, at the furthest edges of the known world. Rome always needed more men, more resources, more money and land, and the British Isles had all of that - and more. It was only a matter of time until the Roman legions would set foot upon Briton shores.

Before the arrival of the Romans in Britain, the island was inhabited by various tribes belonging to the Celtic cultural sphere, collectively known as the Britons. The Britons were a diverse group of people, with different languages, cultures, and social structures. They were organized into various tribal groups, each with its own leaders, customs, and territories. Some of the major tribes included the *Brigantes* in the north, the *Catuvellauni* in the southeast, the *Cornovii* in the west, and the *Iceni* in the east.

The Britons were skilled farmers, raising crops such as wheat, barley, and oats, as well as keeping livestock such as cattle, sheep, and pigs. They also had a strong tradition of metalworking, producing tools, weapons, and jewelry using bronze and iron. For centuries, they were known as capable craftsmen, whose ornamental arts were amongst the finest in the world.

However, the Britons were also very skilled warriors, with a long tradition of inter-tribal warfare. With their ancient traditions focused on war, their lives were often focused on violence and conflict, even if it meant fighting one another. They fought using a variety of weapons, including swords, spears, and shields, and often wore distinctive clothing and body paint, or went completely nude into battle. Simply put, they had a unique character, formed by centuries of cultural exchange between the isles and mainland Europe. The various peoples and cultures that connected in these isles gave birth to a truly illustrious place with unique traditions, cultures, and peoples. By the time the Romans invaded, the Iron Age was already in full swing. This meant that the dominant culture on the isles was that of the Celts, a civilization of Indo-European origins that was formed in Central Europe. Through trade, migration, and cultural exchange, the Celtic culture - and a bit of their people, too - arrived to the British Isles and completely changed its character. From language, customs, practices, and industry - the isles received a totally new face. And over time, distinct tribes formed, each with its own territories and customs. It was these tribes that the invading Romans encountered.

Religion played an important role in Briton society, with many tribes worshiping a pantheon of gods and goddesses associated with nature, war, and fertility. The most famous of these deities was probably the goddess of war and sovereignty, known as Andraste. Nodens, a healing god, was also very popular.

In terms of art and culture, the Britons were known for their intricate metalwork, pottery, and stone carvings. They also had a rich oral tradition of storytelling, with tales of heroes and gods passed down through the generations. Many of these oral traditions survived across centuries, to modern times. Overall, the Britons were a complex and diverse group of people, with a rich history and culture that was shaped by their interactions with each other and with other cultures in the wider Celtic world. All this only made the sudden violent arrival of the Romans all the more worse.

Between 58 and 50 BC, one of Rome's most famous generals, Julius Caesar, was involved in a fierce conquest of the Gallic tribes that lived in what is today France. These were the famed

Gallic Wars, which saw the annexation of the entire land of the Gauls into the Roman Empire. And, as the Britons, who shared cultural traits with the Gauls, were only a stone's throw away, separated by the English Channel, it was inevitable that they too would be subject to attack. In 55 BC, Julius Caesar launched his first attempt to conquer Britain. His expedition consisted of two legions, around 10,000 men, and a large fleet of ships. The Roman forces landed on the coast of Kent, in southeastern Britain, but were immediately met with fierce resistance from the local tribes.

Despite the initial difficulties, Caesar was able to establish a beachhead and marched inland, engaging in several battles with the Britons along the way. However, his forces were eventually forced to withdraw, and Caesar returned to Gaul with all of his troops.

As we see, Rome's first invasion of Britain was largely unsuccessful, with their forces suffering significant casualties and failing to establish a permanent foothold on the island. However, the expedition did provide valuable information about the geography and resources of Britain, and paved the way for future Roman attempts to conquer the island. This was just a probing assault, meant to uncover more information about the tribes that dwelt there, their political situation, and their power.

Caesar did not return to Britain until the following year, in 54 BC, when he launched a second invasion, this time coming prepared, with a larger force. Numerically superior and well-equipped, the Romans were more successful this time, with Caesar claiming to have defeated several tribes and establishing a temporary stronghold on the island. Through sheer power and brute force, he managed to coerce many local tribes to provide him with hostages and tribute, in exchange for peace. He installed client kings loyal to him, and effectively brought Britain into the sphere of Roman influence. Yet even so, he soon departed once again, leaving no Roman troops in Britain. Due to political struggles back in their own home, the Romans were unable to exploit this success and did not return to Britain until a century later.

When they did, they came prepared and bent on fully subjugating the Briton tribes under their rule. The Roman conquest of Britain was a series of military campaigns carried out by the Roman Empire from AD 43 to AD 84, which led to the eventual annexation of most of modern-day England and Wales. In AD 43, the Roman general Aulus Plautius landed with an army of around 40,000 soldiers and began the invasion of Britain. They quickly established a beachhead and marched inland, defeating several Celtic tribes along the way. The Romans soon captured the tribal capital of Camulodunum (modern-day Colchester) and established it as their own capital in the region.

Despite initial successes, the Romans faced significant resistance from the native tribes. The freedom-loving Briton tribes were not keen on suffering beneath the oppressive heel of the Romans, and quickly began formulating plans to regain their lost independence. But for that, they would need a strong leader, and would need to overcome their tribal differences. The person to help them achieve this was Queen Boudica.

Chapter II:
A Regal Woman of War

Cornovii, Dumnonii, Durotriges, Trinovantes, Votadini, Brigantes - these were just some of the numerous tribes that dwelt in Britain. Many shared the same backgrounds and languages, and were connected culturally and religiously. Of these, the Iceni were amongst the most influential. They dwelt in the area of modern East Anglia in England, and were known for their skilled horse riding and metalworking abilities. They had a complex social hierarchy with a ruling class of aristocrats who were responsible for leading the tribe and managing its affairs. They were also known as the Eceni, and their tribal name has roots in the word "Echen", which means "people, tribe, source, origin".

The Iceni, during the conquest of the Romans, were ruled by the powerful King Prasutagus. Prasutagus became king of the Iceni in the mid-1st century AD and was likely one of the eleven kings who formally surrendered to the Roman Emperor Claudius, following the invasion of 43 AD. Seeking to preserve his folk and retain at

least a degree of independence, Prasutagus
formed an alliance with Rome, and was installed
as its client king in the newly formed Roman
province of Britannia. This did give the Iceni
some independence and they managed to retain
their ways, but this would all end soon.
King Prasutagus had a wife, Queen Boudica, and
together they had two daughters. It is said that
the king lived a long and prosperous life, and
died suddenly around 60 AD. Almost instantly,
the Romans ignored their previous agreements
and terminated the independence that the Iceni
enjoyed as a client kingdom. It is unclear why the
Romans broke their agreement with Prasutagus,
but some historians speculate that it may have
been due to his failure to produce a male heir.
Others suggest that the Romans saw an
opportunity to increase their control over the
region and seized it. Either way, the Iceni were
quickly oppressed even more, their nobles lost all
their lands and the region was plundered.

When Prasutagus was gone, his wife Boudica was
left as the sole representative of all their people.
Alas, history does not remember the exact origins

of Boudica. Much of what we know about her early life comes from Roman accounts, which may not be entirely accurate. Still, it is believed that Boudica was born in the late 1st century AD, a daughter of a prominent Iceni nobleman, and it is likely that she received a traditional education and training as a warrior. At the age of 18, Boudica married King Prasutagus, and began her life as the Queen of the Iceni. And from that point on, she gloriously enters the pages of history.

As we mentioned, Boudica had two daughters together with Prasutagus. In the ancient world, a lack of male heirs was always problematic, as direct succession was almost exclusively left upon sons, and not daughters. As old age crept up on Prasutagus, and no sons were born to inherit his semi-independent Kingdom within Britannia, the Romans gradually lost interest in maintaining that independence for the Iceni. With the death of Prasutagus, things quickly soured between the two powers. Historians are not completely certain of the direct causes, but they assume that politically, the Iceni Kingdom was no longer of importance to them. Some sources mention that the actual cause was related to financial loans that the Romans provided to the Iceni. When the former wanted those loans returned, the Iceni refused, believing that they had been repaid through exchange of gifts. Either way, the relationship soon soured, and the Romans were not keen on taking the diplomatic route. Instead, they ravaged the Briton lands. Tacitus, the famed Roman historian, wrote later of the events that unfolded.

According to him, the Romans invaded the small realm of the Iceni, soon after the death of Prasutagus. The countryside was ravaged, the king's own household was completely ransacked, and people abused. But this was not the end of it. To make matters worse, the Romans inflicted a grave injury on the family of the late king - his wife and daughters. Noble Boudica, now the sole representative of the Iceni, was brutally flogged, while her two young daughters were raped. They lived, but the crushing insult and injury could never be erased. The Romans brutally sent their message. Whether the underlying cause to such barbarism was a financial matter, or a simple wish to crush the last remnants of Iceni independence, we might never know. Either way, Boudica was never again the same. So insulted was she, so hurt and shamed, and her daughters horribly humiliated, that nothing else remained but revenge. Her people too, the Iceni, were utterly ravaged, and at once realized that they have lost their freedom - and their traditional way of life - *forever*. Boudica, their queen, would not allow it.

Chapter III:
Boudica Calls Her Banners

Thinking that their message was sent through loud and clear, the Romans departed, focusing now on the other parts of the Briton realm. Their message was sent, certainly, and received clearly. But the Iceni, Boudica at their helm, had a different kind of answer to give them. Almost at once, Queen Boudica began to plot her uprising.

In his famous work "Annals", Roman historian Tacitus tells us that the reason for the revolt was thus:

"Prasutagus, king of the Iceni, after a life of long and renowned prosperity, had made the emperor co-heir with his own two daughters. Prasutagus hoped by this submissiveness to preserve his kingdom and household from attack. But it turned out otherwise. [After his death] kingdom and household alike were plundered like prizes of war, the one by Roman officers, the other by Roman slaves. As a beginning, his widow Boudica was flogged and their daughters raped. The Icenian chiefs were deprived of their hereditary estates as if the

Romans had been given the whole country. The king's own relatives were treated like slaves. And the humiliated Iceni feared still worse, now that they had been reduced to provincial status. So they rebelled."

Needless to say, the Britons were angered, insulted - and ready for *war*. Boudica at once began gathering allies, neighboring Briton tribes who were likewise sick of Roman oppression. Closest to them were the Trinovantes, immediately to the south. The Trinovantes were a tribe likely belonging to the wider group of the Belgae, and dwelt in this area of Britain for several centuries by that time. They had a history of dealing with the Romans, especially during the time of Julius Caesar, but the relationship was never ideal. They too had plenty of reasons to rebel against Rome, and Boudica knew this. They joined up with her forces at once. All together, the Trinovantes and the Iceni had roughly 100,000 warriors at their disposal. They were joined by other oppressed Britons from the region, likely from the tribes such as Catuvellauni and Cantiaci. Their numbers swelled, and some historic sources claim that their army numbered up to 230,000 warriors. Either way, such numbers were immense for this period of history, and the army was undoubtedly formidable.

It is said that on the eve of the rebellion's start, Queen Boudica of the Iceni rode within a war chariot, adorned with her battle equipment, her two daughters in front of her. She paraded before the gathered Briton warriors and chief nobles, numbering many thousands. To them, she gave a powerful and inspirational speech. The Roman historian Cassius Dio, writing many decades afterwards, provides us with a moving speech of Boudica, which she allegedly spoke on that day. He most certainly invented or embellished this speech, as no one was there at the moment to actually capture it in its entirety. If there ever was a speech given by Boudica, it could have been memorized (and then only partially) and passed down orally down the generations. Nevertheless, Dio claims it sounded like this:

"Have we not been robbed entirely of most of our possessions, and those the greatest, while for those that remain we pay taxes? Besides pasturing and tilling for

them all our other possessions, do we not pay a yearly tribute for our very bodies? How much better it would be to have been sold to masters once for all than, possessing empty titles of freedom, to have to ransom ourselves every year! How much better to have been slain and to have perished than to go about with a tax on our heads!... Among the rest of mankind death frees even those who are in slavery to others; only in the case of the Romans do the very dead remain alive for their profit. Why is it that, though none of us has any money (how, indeed, could we, or where would we get it?), we are stripped and despoiled like a murderer's victims? And why should the Romans be expected to display moderation as time goes on, when they have behaved toward us in this fashion at the very outset, when all men show consideration even for the beasts they have newly captured?"

At the time of the start of the revolt, the Roman Governor in Britannia, Gaius Suetonius Paulinus, was busy waging war elsewhere. Around 60-61 AD, he was away conquering the Island of Mona, which is modern-day Anglesey. This island was a refuge of the Britons, and one of their most sacred regions, being a place where their venerable druids lived. Of course, a vast number of Roman soldiers that were stationed in Britannia were engaged in this conquest, allowing the rebels of Boudica to organize their efforts largely unobstructed. But even so, time was of the essence, and it seems that Boudica and her commanders did not establish any detailed plan of attack. According to Cassius Dio's writings, Boudica employed a form of a divination ritual, in order to deduce the best direction of attack. The ritual involved her hiding a hare within the folds of her dress - when the hare was released, the direction in which it fled was interpreted and seen as an omen. Likewise, the Britons invoked goddess Andraste, calling for victory in war.

Chapter IV:
The War Begins

The hare ran towards Camulodunum. This was the first target of the rebellious army of Boudica, and it's possible that it would have been even if the hare ran elsewhere. Camulodunum, known today as Colchester, was the former capital of the Trinovantes tribe. It was, however, "commandeered" by the Romans, who made it a provincial capital, a *castrum* and a *colonia* for the discharged veterans of Roman wars. A vast temple was built there, dedicated to the former emperor, Claudius. No longer was this the town of brave Trinovantes - it was wholly Romanized and the locals were repeatedly mistreated by the veteran soldiers. It was only natural that Boudica and her warriors would want to free it from that oppression.

The attack of the Britons on Camulodunum was totally unexpected. They descended upon the city with all their might, causing widespread panic amongst the Roman populace and plundering without mercy or hesitation. Destruction seemed inevitable, and the population sought reinforcements from the *procurator* of Britannia, Catus Decianus, who only sent them two hundred auxiliary troops. It was this same Catus Decianus whose arrogant actions partly - or wholly - caused the revolt of the Britons. He was the one demanding the return of loans with interest, and his troops and slaves that plundered the Iceni court and humiliated Boudica and her daughters. Seeing that his actions caused a violent revolt, Decianus promptly fled across the channel to Gaul.

Camulodunum did not stand a chance. Archeological evidence shows that the Britons methodically destroyed the city completely, burning and sacking in their anger. The same thing was written by Tacitus. At the time, with the bulk of the Roman forces being away at Mona, the only considerable force in the area belonged to Quintus Petillius Cerialis, the future governor of Britannia. He was commanding the forces of Legio IX *Hispana,* and rushed in an attempt to relieve the city. Known as a bold and capable commander, he nevertheless failed to defeat the Britons that were vastly numerically superior. We learn that the warriors descended on the Roman legionaries, killing every single one that was on the battlefield. Quintus Petillius suffered an overwhelming defeat, lost all of his troops, and barely escaped alive with a few cavalrymen. In Camulodunum, the last few survivors holed themselves up in the vast Temple of Claudius, where they were besieged and after two days assaulted and decimated. With that, Camulodunum fell.

The Britons sent a clear message of their own. They were not willing to stand idly and see their lands ravaged and their people oppressed. With warrior queen Boudica at their helm, they proved that they had the strength in numbers and that they had no mercy left in their hearts. The most important Briton statement was the utter destruction of the Temple of Claudius. Extravagant and rich, the temple was the symbol of Roman presence in Britannia, the emblem of their power and prestige. It was erected at the expense of the oppressed Britons, and was to them a symbol of Roman domination. When Boudica razed it to the ground, the people rejoiced, while the Romans suddenly became aware that they were dealing with a serious and powerful enemy.

It was important for Boudica too. According to the Roman historians, this Iceni queen had the appearance of a true noble Briton woman. She was tall and well-built, proportionate and powerful. Her red-auburn hair and her lavish battle dress left a lasting impression on any follower or enemy, and she quickly became a symbol for all Britons - a true leader and a freedom-loving woman of war. Even her name carried great symbolism: according to modern research, the name Boudica (also spelled as Boadicea), is made up from Brythonic words *boudi (victory, win) and *-ka (having) suffix. Thus, quite literally, her name means "Victorious Woman". Driven by rage and the desire for freedom, blind to the dangers of war and thirsty for Roman blood, Boudica boldly stepped up in front of her warriors and vowed not to stop until their realm was free. Here, it is important to note that in the society of Ancient Britons, gender played a less important role. A great leader of armies could be either a man or a woman, receiving equal respect and adoration. And Boudica had both.

In the meantime, the news of destroyed Camulodunum reached governor Gaius Suetonius Paulinus, the leader of the Roman armies that were off conquering Anglesey. Alarmed by the magnitude of Briton's destruction, and upon hearing that the provincial capital was simply *no more*, he quickly gathered his Legio IX Hispana and marched eastwards, through territory filled with Briton tribes who were quickly growing unrestful. Here, Suetonius Paulinus had to thoroughly think through his next steps. It was clear to him that the Briton force would march from Camulodunum to the next big Roman settlement, which was Londinium (the future London). Londinium was a relatively new settlement, formed around 43 AD, and had a different character to Camulodunum. It was not a fortified *castrum* per se, but rather a regional center of commerce and administration. It had a population of Roman officials, as well as merchants and craftsmen. Tacitus tells us that *"Londinium, which, though undistinguished by the name of a colony, was much frequented by a number of merchants and trading vessels."*

All this meant that the city was an easy target, and carried plenty of loot for an enemy force. What is more, it was poorly defended, with the bulk of Roman forces being with Paulinus. The decision ahead was quite difficult.

From the Roman chroniclers we also learn that the Briton warriors had a nasty reputation. War was a big part of their culture, so they never shied away from it. Here we learn thus:

"The natives (Britons) enjoy plundering and think of nothing else. Bypassing forts and garrisons, they made for where loot was richest and protection weakest. Roman and provincial deaths at the places mentioned are estimated at seventy thousand. For the British did not take or sell prisoners, or practice other war time exchanges. They could not wait to cut throats, hang, burn, and crucify - as though avenging, in advance, the retribution that was on its way."

Through this passage, we see that the wrath of the Britons was unlike anything the Romans experienced before. These warriors did not hesitate to inflict grievous death upon ordinary citizens of the Roman province of Britannia, and this caused great fear of them. Paulinus knew this all too well, but could not rush to battle. He knew, after all, that he was vastly outnumbered. If he'd make the same mistake as Quintus Petrillius Cerialis, who was utterly crushed at Camulodunum, Paulinus could lose all his warriors. Thus, he decided that it was in his best interests to sacrifice Londinium to the Briton war party, and instead withdrew to regroup his forces and to - literally - save the entire province.

Thus it was that Londinium and its folk were left to their grim fate. He turned a blind eye to the calls for aid, and would not risk an all-out defeat. Those that could and wished, fled from the city and joined him as refugees. Those that could not leave, however, were subjected to a grisly death. Boudica's Britons flooded the city, causing widespread death and destruction. They slew all that stood in their path. Modern archeological research, centered on Roman Londinium, shows a distinct layer of absolute destruction. Human bones and heads were discovered in contemporary layers, indicating that the fate of the city was indeed shocking. The Roman historian Tacitus described the attack in his book "Annals":

"The Iceni, and others of the Britons, with a determination which spoke more of revenge than of plunder or of booty, spared neither man, woman nor child, nor even sacred buildings."

The attack was brutal, with many of the town's inhabitants killed or taken captive, and buildings and temples destroyed. It was a hefty price that Paulinus had to pay in order to stay in the fight. But Boudica's determination did not falter. She was bent on revenge and independence, that she would not shy away from plunder and massacre. She was a woman of war, and her life was now all about *victory or death.*

Chapter V:
A Duel of the Fates

The Britons were now on a decisive path of war. They would not stop until revenge was complete. After Camulodunum and Londinium, they continued on their destructive path towards Verulamium. This bustling Roman city is today known as St. Albans, and lies some 20 miles (32 km) north-west of London. It was upon the historic Watling Street route, and as such presented a ripe prize for the Britons, standing right on their path. Again, the destruction was unparalleled. Tacitus says that *"The army of Boadicea fell upon the town of Verulamium. The place was fired and plundered, and the inhabitants slaughtered like sheep."* The temple of Mercury was a particular target for Boudica's forces, as it was a symbol of Roman power and authority in the town. They set it alight and destroyed it, along with many other buildings. The attack on Verulamium was a significant moment in Boudica's rebellion, as it demonstrated the weakness of Roman rule in the face of determined opposition. The town was left in ruins, and its inhabitants were either killed or taken captive. It too was a bustling Roman town, built upon the previous capital of the Catuvellauni tribe, known then as Verlamio.

Seeing the devastation that Boudica and her followers were capable of, Gaius Paulinus knew that a decisive battle would have to be fought soon, or else the chain of destruction would continue unabated, and he would be powerless to stop it.

Here we have to note the darker side of the Ancient Britons, and their insatiable thirst for vengeance. In their revolt, and their attack on three Roman cities, they did not spare anyone, regardless of age or sex. Romans, considered at the time pioneers of civilization and advanced technologies, were largely appalled by the warlike behavior. This is why their chroniclers and scholars wrote about these events with so much disgust and from a biased stance. But it is no secret that the Britons - just like the Gauls and all other cultures that the Romans dubbed "barbarian" - committed ghastly massacres. In their eyes, and in their cultures, these killings were not seen as a controversy. They saw death and pain in a different light. Still, many Romans and Britons who were allied to them, perished at the hands of Boudica's followers - and in terrible ways. Many of these ordinary citizens were slaughtered in unimaginable ways, and were often sacrificed to pagan gods. Even decades before, in 9 AD, we hear of Germanic shamans and druids sacrificing captive Roman soldiers in sacred groves, during the famed Battle of Teutoburg Forest. Returning to the site of that famed battle decades later, Roman legionnaires saw heaps of bleached bones of their predecessors fallen in battle.

Similar practices existed decades later, especially amongst the peoples belonging to the Celtic cultural group. For centuries, the Celts' culture was oriented towards a patriarchal society and warfare. There existed an emphasized tradition of trophy hunting amongst the Celts, especially head-hunting. Celtic warriors would often cut off the feet of the warriors they had slain, believing that this would prevent them from walking over to the afterlife. These warlike traditions, paired with the anger that they felt, compelled the

Britons to spare no person they encountered, often killing them in ways that were deemed brutal by the Romans who possessed a different cultural background.

As we said, Gaius Suetonius was fully aware of the decisions he was making. He left Londinium and Verulamium to their fates, sacrificing them in order to regroup his forces and have a fighting chance. He amassed a considerable army, composed of the entire Legio XIV Gemina which was under his command, as well as portions of Legio XX Valeria Victrix, and many available auxiliary troops. Furthermore, he gave the order to Poenius Postumus, the prefect of Legio II Augusta which was stationed at Isca (modern Exeter) to rush and bring his troops - but the man disobeyed the order and did not come. Still, Gaius Suetonius Paulinus had at his command some 10,000 soldiers, some experienced and some not, which he had to use to the best of his abilities in order for the revolt of Boudica to be quelled. This would be no easy task, he knew, since the warrior queen of the Iceni had at her command a vast horde of warriors, which numbered up to

300,000, according to ancient Roman sources. Tthis number is likely exaggerated, but even so, Boudica must have had at least 100,000 warriors at her disposal, and it is more than certain that all oppressed Britons from the region flocked to her side, both men and women, all who were capable of fighting. Paulinus would need a miracle in order to crush such a force - but the only thing he had at his disposal was his resolve and his tactician's mind. So, he began searching for a battle site. Soon enough, Boudica moved to meet him, and the two armies opposed one another, ready to battle. What ensued was the decisive moment of Boudica's revolt, the clash that is today known as the Battle of Watling Street. Tacitus tells us:

"Suetonius collected the fourteenth brigade (or legion) and detachments of the twentieth, together with the nearest available auxiliaries - amounting to nearly ten thousand armed men - and decided to attack without further delay. He chose a position in a defile with a wood behind him. There could be no enemy he knew, except at his front, where there was open country without cover for ambushes. Suetonius drew up his

regular troops in close order, with the light-armed
auxiliaries at their flanks, and the cavalry massed on
the wings. On the British side, cavalry and infantry
bands seethed over a wide area in unprecedented
numbers. Their confidence was such that they brought
their wives with them to see the victory, installing
them in carts stationed on the edge of the battlefield."

It must have been an exceptional sight for the average Roman soldier present: seeing across the battlefield and witnessing a vast flood of vicious Briton warriors who were out for vengeance and bent on the complete destruction of the Roman army. The courage of ancient warriors had to be exceptional at the time.

Still, a soldier's duty was placing trust into the commanding general. They had to believe that the decisions they were making were right. And the decisions that Gaius Paulinus made were marked with the cunning of a seasoned Roman general. He ordered his men to be positioned in a defile, just as Tacitus says, where a forest stood at their back, preventing encirclement or an attack from the rear. The defile which he chose gave him some protection from the sides too, and greatly narrowed the battlefield. It was a shrewd choice, one that was obviously well-planned. What is more, the wide open plain that stretched in front prevented any sort of surprises or ambushes from the Britons - everything was *plain* to see. The only way Boudica could conduct an attack was from the front, and within a gradually narrowing battlefield. This meant that the numerical superiority that she possessed did not mean much under such circumstances.

At this point, the historical accounts clearly point out that Gaius Suetonius Paulinus possessed one key advantage - experience. As early as 40 AD - some twenty years before Boudica's revolt - he entered the pages of history as the governor of Mauretania, and almost immediately he was involved in a suppression of a local rebellion. In the following year, he became the first Roman commander to lead his troops across the Atlas Mountains. Thus, from 40 to 60 AD, Paulinus forged his experience across the vast Roman Empire, and became one of its most capable commanders. Now, facing Boudica, he had plenty of seniority to benefit from, and the positioning of his army clearly shows this.

And so it was that the revolt of Queen Boudica came to this decisive big battle. Tacitus, writing more than 50 years after the revolt, tells us in his histories that the leaders of both armies gave inspirational speeches to their respective forces, hoping to boost morale. Reportedly, Boudica mounted her war chariot, her daughters beside her, and she rode before the army saying this:

"'But now,' she said, 'it is not as a woman descended from noble ancestry, but as one of the people that I am avenging lost freedom, my scourged body, the outraged chastity of my daughters. Roman lust has gone so far that not our very persons, nor even age or virginity, are left unpolluted. But heaven is on the side of a righteous vengeance; a legion which dared to fight has perished; the rest are hiding themselves in their camp, or are thinking anxiously of flight. They will not sustain even the din and the shout of so many thousands, much less our charge and our blows. If you weigh well the strength of the armies, and the causes of the war, you will see that in this battle you must conquer or die. This is a woman's resolve; as for men, they may live and be slaves.'

Ever since, historians doubted the accuracy of this speech. It is almost impossible that someone who was present "wrote" the speech down to save it for posterity. While there is a strong possibility that Boudica did address her troops, the exact contents of her speech remain lost to history. What Tacitus wrote was likely an imagination, a fictional speech that served to present Boudica in a certain light.

But he also presents us with the speech that Gaius Suetonius Paulinus gave to his legionaries. And, in stark contrast to Boudica's speech, this one seems oddly realistic. It is blunt, soldierly, and practical, which is the likely way it sounded. And, considering that Tacitus's father-in-law, Gnaeus Julius Agricola (the future governor of Britain) was present on the staff of Suetonius at the time, he could have reported the speech fairly accurately. What Gaius Suetonius Paulinus said was memorized thus:

> *"Ignore the racket made by these savages. There are more women than men in their ranks. They are not soldiers — they are not even properly equipped. We*

The speech is straight to the point, as soldierly as could be. It tells the legionaries what should be done, and *how* to do it. Interestingly, Paulinus mentions that *"they are not even properly equipped"*. Now, how well were Boudica's soldiers equipped? Could they have matched a Roman legionary? An important historical fact gives us the ideal answer. Several years preceding the revolt of Boudica, the subjugated Briton tribes were systematically relieved of their weapons. In order for the Romans to successfully rule over Britannia, they had to rid the common folk from their weaponry. This they did - it took a bit of time, but tribe after tribe was devoid of their best weapons, in order to reduce their fighting ability and to suppress the chances of rebellion. Remember that, at the time, quality swords and deadly weapons were a sought after possession, and not everyone could afford them and own them. The poorest and simplest of Briton soldiers likely never even held a true iron sword - they were most likely equipped with cudgels, maces, spears, and makeshift weaponry.

Modern historians thus commonly agree that Boudica's army was noticeably poorly equipped, especially when compared to the Roman legionaries who were the most modern warriors on the battlefield at the time. A Roman soldier possessed extensive training, and - more than likely - plenty of combat experience. What also gave them an edge was the tactics and battle concepts that they were taught from the start. This was no loose formation of warriors: this was a killing machine synchronized to perfection. And their weaponry, too, was top notch. They carried short throwing spears, called the *pilum*, long rectangular shields that protected most of their exposed body, helmets and armor, and deadly short swords called *gladius* - all this made them exceptionally deadly.

On the other hand, the warriors of Boudica were likely a different sight. Ancient Roman sources tell us that the Britons had something of a *berserker* type of warrior. They would fall into a battle frenzy and fight completely nude, wearing naught but their golden *torcs*, special necklaces. Painted with tribal tattoos, they were certainly a fear-inducing sight on the battlefield. But they lacked any protection whatsoever. Those warriors that did not fight nude likely lacked any substantial armor, and did not possess advanced battle tactics or fighting methods. And thus it was, even though Boudica had thousands of men and women at her disposal, they still lacked the modernity and skill that the Romans had.

Gaius Suetonius Paulinus knew this all too well, which is reflected in his stark and blunt speech. He entered the Battle at Watling Street with unparalleled confidence and composure, ready to "do or die". The confidence of the commander certainly "rubbed off" on the troops, and the Roman legionaries were eager to fight, even though they faced an incredible multitude of Briton warriors. So, without further hesitation, Gaius Paulinus gave the signal for battle.

The fate of Britannia was being decided upon.

Chapter VI:
Boudica at the Helm

The Roman trumpets sounded the *attack.* And the Britons rushed to answer that call. The Roman legionnaires moved in a tightly packed formation, not running nor walking, but rather inching forward at a steady and calculated pace. The Britons, however, rushed forward in a great, unruly mass of warriors, confident in their overwhelming numbers and eager to spill Roman blood. But the disadvantages were soon to show. Were this battle fought on a wide open plain, the Romans would certainly be crushed decisively. But Gaius Suetonius Paulinus knew this all too well, and thus chose his location with the shrewdness of an aged tactician.

The gradually narrowing battlefield, constrained by the edges of a shallow defile, meant that the Britons could not utilize their great numbers. Their swelling ranks were "funneled", meaning that a majority of the warriors could not be effectively used.

The Roman general placed his limited number of cavalry at his flanks, with the lightly-armed auxiliaries close to them. In the center were the deadly formations of legionaries. Seeing the Britons charging at them on foot, they received the orders to let loose their missiles. The short throwing spears flew with deadly precision and dazzling speed, cutting down hundreds of warriors at once. And again, they threw their second spears, with the same result. Only then, when their missiles were exhausted, did they receive the order to move.

Here we need to understand that the Roman soldiers were the unparalleled masters of close quarter fighting. Their tactics allowed that only the front row of soldiers was engaged in battle at one time. Their shields guarding their bodies, and the shields of the other soldiers guarding their heads, these men could perform short and precise stabs to the front, systematically removing enemies. As the front row tired, it was quickly replaced with the second row in line, and so the cycle went on. Always a fresh line of troops, and always the same deadly stabs. The effectiveness of such a tactic was unquestionable.

Now, when the order was given, the Romans marched forward in a wedge formation. The cavalry advanced on the flanks, essentially circling the stunned Britons. At this moment, Boudica and her warriors realized the terrible position in which they found themselves. The carts and chariots which they brought now prevented their escape. Tacitus describes the grisly scenes as follows:

"At first, the legionaries stood motionless, keeping to the defile as a natural protection: then, when the closer advance of the enemy had enabled them to exhaust their missiles with certitude of aim, they dashed forward in a wedge-like formation. The auxiliaries charged in the same style; and the cavalry, with lances extended, broke a way through any parties of resolute men whom they encountered. The remainder took to flight, although escape was difficult, as the cordon of wagons had blocked the outlets. The troops gave no quarter even to the women: the baggage animals themselves had been speared and added to the pile of bodies. The glory won in the course of the day was remarkable, and equal to that of our older victories: for, by some accounts, little less than eighty thousand Britons fell, at a cost of some four hundred Romans killed and a not much greater number of wounded."

It is likely that the battle was a quick and bloody affair. The initial stages stunned the Britons that were taken at a disadvantage. As the spear showers turned into brutal close quarter fighting, they soon realized that they can't be as effective as they could be, given the narrowing battlefield. The cavalry harassed their flanks, and all in all, the casualties mounted with dazzling speed. Seeing all your allied warriors falling dead all around was certainly bad for morale. The Britons soon decided that the retreat was the best option. But their escape routes were blocked - by their own wagons! It was a deadly flaw that Boudica sadly overlooked. Her army was now essentially trapped, left at the mercy of the Roman warriors. And, sadly, there was no mercy to spare. What ensued was a gruesome massacre, a bloodshed on a scale that was never before seen in that realm. Having first decimated the attacking Britons with their javelins, the Romans now proceeded to systematically cut them down in throngs. Their close quarter advance had deadly effectiveness - Britons were slain en masse, without regard to their gender. Historical sources say that the casualties were incredibly high, and most of them were deaths. The Britons could not easily escape, and were thus simply cut down as they milled about. Any and all attempts at escape were pointless. Interestingly, the sources state that the wrath of the Romans was such that they did not even spare the pack animals that were a part of that chaos. Anything and everything that moved was slain at the spot.

The Battle of Watling Street was a clear, decisive, and above all *brutal* victory for the seasoned general Gaius Suetonius Paulinus. It cemented his reputation as a capable commander, and brought unparalleled glory to his legionaries. Their fame was such that Poenius Postumus, the commander who refused to march his own troops to aid in the battle, promptly killed himself because of the glory he failed to be a part of.

"Poenius Postumus, chief of staff of the second division which had not joined Suetonius, learning of the success of the other two formations, stabbed himself to death because he had cheated his formation of its share in the victory and broken regulations by disobeying his commander's orders."

The victory of the Romans was achieved with minimal losses. Some 400 fallen Roman soldiers are reported, against an incredible number of up to 80,000 Briton casualties. Needless to say, modern historians take this number with a grain of salt, as it was most likely blown out of proportion in order to emphasize the glory of the Romans. Yet, even so, the number of British dead was most certainly incredibly high, numbering in the tens of thousands. It was an incredible blow on the Iceni and the local tribes, whose warriors were brutally decimated. The battle was a complete failure on their part.

Today, the exact site of this battle remains a mystery. Roman histories gave only vague directions to the position, and several possible sites are known today. Most modern historians favor potential location sites in the Midlands, probably along the Roman road which became Watling Street. Watling Street was a major Roman "highway" that connected Londinium (London) with Viroconium (Wroxeter) and other important towns in Britannia. It is believed to have run in a roughly southeast to northwest direction, crossing the southern part of the island. The road's route has been identified in several places, but the specific section relevant to the battle remains disputed.

One prevalent theory suggests that the Battle of Watling Street occurred somewhere near the modern-day town of High Cross in Leicestershire, England. This location is considered a strong candidate due to its strategic position along Watling Street and its proximity to known Roman settlements and military sites. Another proposed site for the battle is the ancient Manduessedum, known today as Mancetter, near Atherstone in Warwickshire. This location is also situated on Watling Street and has some supporting archaeological evidence, such as Roman artifacts and earthworks. However, it is important to note that the exact location of the battle has not been definitively established. The lack of precise information about the Battle of Watling Street's site is partly due to the limited historical records from that time. The primary written accounts of the battle come from Roman historians Tacitus and Cassius Dio, but their descriptions do not provide sufficient details to pinpoint the exact location.

Chapter VII:
The Warrior Queen's Demise

The brightest flames are often the quickest to go out. And like a bright torch to light the path to freedom, Boudica and her revolt were gone all too quickly. Overly confident in their capabilities, and funneled cluelessly into a tactician's perfectly picked battlefield, the freedom-fighting Britons were decisively crushed. Sadly, there is a lot of information that has slipped through the fingers of time. All that we know is based on somewhat impoverished accounts of Roman historians that wrote several decades after the revolt. That is why there is plenty about Boudica and her revolt that historians simply do not know.

But we do know that her fight for independence and justice struck fear into the heart of the Roman Emperor himself. Gaius Suetonius Tranquillus, an important Roman historian, calls Boudica's revolt a "crisis", and claims that it was so serious that it almost persuaded Emperor Nero to completely abandon Britain. Initially, we can understand his position: he desperately lacked troops in Britannia, and was facing a vast army of Britons who were ready to lay waste to every Roman town in the region. But it was the decisive move of General Gaius Paulinus that saved the day. Sadly, some of the most important aspects of this crisis remain lost to us, specifically - the ultimate fate of Warrior Queen Boudica. The ancient sources diverge on this important information. For example, Tacitus tells us that Boudica, defeated and disheartened, barely escaped the site of the battle and then committed suicide by poisoning herself. She did so in order to avoid capture. If she had fallen into the hands of the Romans, she would have certainly been carried back to Rome and paraded in a *triumph* ceremony, after which she'd be killed. It would have brought even more shame on the defeated Britons. So, there is a strong possibility that Boudica, not wishing to see their kinsfolk further shamed, selflessly took her own life.

But, again, this claim by Tacitus cannot be confirmed.

Even more confusion arises from the later account by Cassius Dio. This Roman historian tells us simply that Boudica fell ill not long after the defeat, and soon after died. After her death, the

Britons provided her with a lavish burial. In this account there are also indications that the Britons were initially not dissuaded by their catastrophic defeat, and planned to fight again.

> *"Nevertheless, not a few made their escape and were preparing to fight again. In the meantime, however, Boudica fell sick and died. The Britons mourned her deeply and gave her a costly burial; but, feeling that now at last they were really defeated, they scattered to their homes. So much for affairs in Britain."*

Either one of these ancient claims could be true. Some contemporary claims speak of a great famine that ravaged Britannia at the time, greatly affecting the Briton tribes. This, together with the great defeat, could have been the final subduing of the Iceni and their allied tribes. What is more, the mention of Boudica's lavish burial inspired many archaeologists and amateur explorers to go searching for her final resting place. Needless to say, none of them were successful, and no known archeological site can be linked to the burial place of the Iceni queen.

Simply put, the final fate of this brave woman of war remains a historical mystery.

Taking precautionary measures against further possible uprisings, Emperor Nero was quick to bring new changes into Britannia. Immediately following his great victory at Watling Street, General Gaius Suetonius Paulinus wanted to utilize the situation and forever quell the Britons. He conducted widespread harsh punitive operations against the native populace, causing further death and suffering. His immediate actions were not welcome: the new governor in Britannia, Gaius Julius Alpinus Classicianus was quick to condemn this harshness, fearing new unrest amongst the Britons. This criticism from Classicianus was quickly noted by the Emperor, who sent his agent Polyclitus to investigate. Ultimately, fearing that the harshness of Paulinus would cause further unrest amongst the Briton tribes, Nero had him replaced with the more moderate Publius Petronius Turpilianus. Nevertheless, the significance of Gaius Suetonius Paulinus' victory was not forgotten, and he gained even more renown amongst his peers.

Alas, while the Roman bout of fear was quick to pass, and they continued to revel in their victory, the fate of the Britons was much, much darker. Their brave warrior queen, having stood up for all their rights, was dead. It is quite likely that both her daughters perished too, either in the battle or after it. History does not mention their fate at any point, but it is unlikely they survived. Either way, Boudica's fate was altogether tragic. From the death of her husband, to the insults to her kingdom, and all the way to the degradation that she and her daughters endured - this brave woman of war had to struggle through a life of tragedy and pain. But instead of submitting to the Romans and letting this fate run over her, Boudica rose up against all odds, and lit the flame of freedom in the hearts of the Britons. And it is this choice, and her bravery, that reminds of the fierceness and the bravery of the Ancient Briton tribes, and how women stood equally besides men, in both peace and war.

Conclusion

Even though Boudica's fight was short-lived, lasting no more than a year, it nevertheless left lasting traces on the forming society of Britain. Her selfless sacrifice resounded through the ages, inspiring men and women for centuries that came. After the Romans departed, several centuries after Boudica's rebellion, the new, Romano-British society was left all on its own, vulnerable and facing new and eager conquerors. Later down the line, the realms of the Anglo-Saxons faced their own terrible threats, and so did all the subsequent realms of Britain. And in all those times of need and desperation, when the desire for freedom and independence was at its highest, the peoples of Britain could look back to the story of Boudica, a fierce woman of war, and find in themselves that all-important spark of courage. Even in modern times, when the story of Boudica was not much more than very distant history, people could draw inspiration from it. Her tale and her sacrifice became a symbol for the oppressed women of the modern times. She inspired the feminists of the British Suffrage movement, who fought - indirectly - for greater rights for women. To them, it was a stark comparison: women in modern ages had less rights than did the women in 60 AD Roman Britannia. These women, persevering in their cause and fighting for their personal rights, were the Boudica's of our age, fighting with equal zeal. A pamphlet from the Brighton Society of the National Union of Women's Suffrage Societies (NUWSS), released in January 1909, mentions Boudica as an inspiration, writing of her thus:

"... this heroic figure of a woman, mother, and ruler ... represents a type of the "eternal feminine" – the guardian of the hearth, the avenger of its wrongs upon the defacer and the despoiler."

Of course, her actions in 61 AD had immediate consequences as well. Considering that her revolt only involved a select few tribes of the region closest to the Iceni, we can safely assume that many of the other tribes that were not involved looked with expectation at the outcome of the revolt. Some of these tribes were allied to Rome, perhaps only nominally, while others were eager to be rid of them. If Boudica's revolt succeeded, and they all rose up to arms, what fate would have come to Britannia? And would its future be totally changed?

Sadly, we will never know. The other tribes, seeing Boudica defeated so terribly, quickly abandoned the idea of rebelling. Of course, some followed in Boudica's footsteps, mounting revolts of their own. Southern Britain was for the most part pacified, following the Roman victory at Watling Street, but Northern Britain still remained a restless and volatile place. So it was that, 69 AD, just a few years after Boudicca, a brave chief of the Brigantes tribe called Venutius, mounted a revolt of his own, with mixed results. There is no doubt that he - at least in part - followed the example that the Queen of Iceni left before.

Either way, we can safely say that Boudica was a woman without an equal during her time. A true freedom fighter, she stood before her own people not as a slighted noble, but as a common woman, whose freedom and rights were brutally taken away. As such, she attracted the common folk, those most vulnerable to the harsh policies of the Romans.

In the end, we come face to face with the profound legacy left behind by a warrior queen who dared to defy the forces of the largest empire in the world. Boudicca's story, intertwined with the struggle for freedom and the resilience of the human spirit, resonates far beyond the pages of history.

As we reflect upon her tumultuous journey, we are confronted with the timeless questions that echo through the ages. What drives individuals to rise against tyranny? What fuels the flames of revolution within the hearts of those who have been wronged? And perhaps most importantly, what is the true cost of defiance?

Boudica's rebellion, with its triumphs and its ultimate defeat, reminds us that the path to justice is often paved with sacrifice and suffering. Her indomitable spirit, the rallying cry that united tribes, and the relentless pursuit of a better world stand as testament to the strength of a woman who refused to be silenced. May the echoes of Boudicca's war cry continue to resonate, awakening the warrior within each of us, and inspiring generations to come.

References:

Fraser, A. 1999. *The Warrior Queens: Boadicea's Chariot.* London: Arrow.

Grant, M. 1988. *Tacitus: The Annals of Imperial Rome. Translated.* Penguin Books.

Unwin, C. and Hingley, R. 2006. *Boudica: Iron Age Warrior Queen.* A&C Black.

Unknown. *The Life of Boudicca: The Warrior Queen of the Iceni.* History. [Online] Available at:

Note to the reader

Thank you for taking the time to enjoy the story of Boudica. While much of her story has been lost to time, we have tried to be faithful to her plight and bold bravery. Feel free to continue the series as we continue looking into the brave women of history. If you truly have enjoyed hearing about them, don't just leave a review, tell others about them.

Teaser

Joan of Arc
Women of War - Book 2

In the annals of history, a select few exist whose lives transcend the boundaries of time and inspire generations to come. Joan of Arc, an extraordinary figure who emerged from tumultuous medieval France, is undeniably one such luminary. In this captivating retelling of her life and deeds, we will embark on an inspirational and enlightening journey, exploring the legacy and the indomitable spirit of this remarkable young woman who defied societal norms and changed the course of history.

Joan lived during the fifteenth century, an era characterized by turmoil and conflict, and the fated duel between two giants - France and England. From that giant war, a single person rose, towering high above it - Joan of Arc. Her story captivates the imagination like no other. Born in the humble village of Domrémy, she hailed from a modest background, seemingly destined for a life of obscurity, but fate had other plans. Joan's profound devotion to her faith, combined with a relentless determination, catapulted her from the fringes of society into the tumultuous world of war, politics, and spiritual fervor.

In this genuinely fascinating account of her life, we aim to shed light on the historical enigma that was Joan of Arc. Drawing upon historical records and the writings of famed contemporary chroniclers, we weave together a tapestry of her extraordinary achievements. So let us delve deep into the annals of war-torn medieval Europe as we bring to life the intricate chaos of politics, religion, and conflict. This chaos formed the backdrop against which Joan's epic tale unfolded. Was she indeed a messenger of God, as she so fervently believed, or an extraordinary individual caught in the throes of a turbulent era?

www.ingramcontent.com/pod-product-compliance
Lightning Source LLC
Chambersburg PA
CBHW021349160726

47994CB00007B/2891